Desert Clowns
Katacha Díaz

Rigby

Roadrunners are birds that like to travel
on the ground.
They run along the road.
That is how they got their name!

The roadrunner is a funny-looking bird.
It is a different kind of bird, too.
Even though it's a bird, it doesn't fly well.
When it does, it can only fly for a short time.

The roadrunner lives in the desert.
It is found in the southwestern United States.
Roadrunners also live in the countryside
in Mexico.

The Mexican people believe
that roadrunners bring good luck!
They call the birds *correcaminos*.
This means a bird that runs along the road.

Roadrunners have brown feathers.
Their feathers look like the colors of the desert.
That makes roadrunners hard to see!

The roadrunner has a long tail.
It's almost as long as its body.

Roadrunners like eating and playing together.
They look silly when they walk
with their tail in the air.

They have orange and blue skin
behind their eyes.
People call them the clowns of the desert!

The roadrunner's feet
are strong and powerful.
It has two toes in front and
two toes behind.

2 miles an hour

Roadrunners are fast birds.
They can run as fast
as 15 miles an hour!
Their tracks leave X s
in the dust.

8 miles an hour

15 miles an hour

The roadrunner has good eyesight
and hearing.
Its beak is strong and sharp for hunting.

The roadrunner hunts to get food.
It eats snakes, lizards, insects, and spiders.
It drinks water from plants and rain puddles.
Life in the desert is not easy
for the roadrunner!

New Mexico is one of the desert states
where the roadrunner lives.
The people there chose it as the state bird.

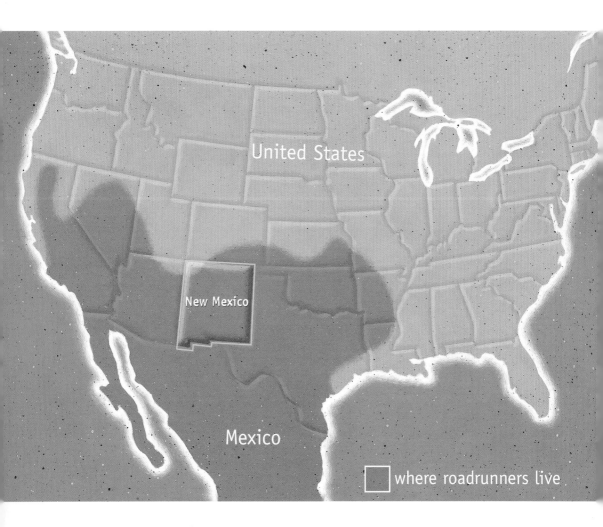

They love to watch these desert clowns have fun!

Index

❯ What is a roadrunner?. 2–3

❯ Where does the roadrunner live?. . . . 4–5

❯ What does the roadrunner look like?. . 6–9

❯ How fast is the roadrunner?. 10–11

❯ What does the roadrunner eat?. . . . 12–13

❯ Why is the roadrunner special
in New Mexico?. 14–15